LACED

Sam Mueller

BROADWAY PLAY PUBLISHING INC
New York
www.broadwayplaypublishing.com
info@broadwayplaypublishing.com

LACED

First edition: December 2024
I S B N: 979-8-88856-046-4

Book design: Marie Donovan
Page make-up: Adobe InDesign
Typeface: Palatino

The world premiere of LACED was produced by About Face Theater (Megan Carney, Artistic Director) in Chicago, opening on 25 March 2022 at The Den Theater. The cast and creative contributors were:

AUDRA .... Mariah Copeland
MINNOW .... Daniela Martinez
CAT .... Collin Quinn Rice

understudies:
AUDRA .... Caitlin Dobbins
MINNOW .... Jalbelly Guzmán
CAT .... Ricki Romano

Director .... Lexi Saunders
Production Manager .... Audrey Kleine
Choreographer/Assistant Director .... Jacinda Ratcliffe
Dramaturg .... Hannah Herrera Greenspan
Production Stage Manager .... Amalie Vega
Assistant Stage Manager .... Becky Valek
Dialect Coach .... Sándor Menéndez
Intimacy Consultant .... Kirsten Baity
Scenic Design Advisor .... Regina Garcia
Scenic Designer .... Sydney Lynn
Technical Director .... Alan Weusthoff
Scenic Painter .... Altman Art Haus
Costume Designer .... Jos N Banks
Props Designer .... Caitlin McCarthy
Sound Designer .... Thomas Dixon
Associate Sound Designer .... Ariel Zetina
Lighting Designer .... Heather Sparling
Lead Electrician .... Ben Carne
Graphic Designer .... Charles Riffenburg
Spanish Translators ..... Pauline Moll & Sándor Menéndez

CHARACTERS & SETTING

they're all queer.

MINNOW, *she/her/hers, Cuban-American*
tattooed & pierced, probably wearing combat boots

CAT, *they/them/theirs, non-binary, white*
witch femme drag extraordinaire

AUDRA, *she/her/hers, Black*
newest to the weekend night shift

Place:
The Beacon—a queer bar in Tampa, Florida
a little dive-y

Time:
the days before the 2016 election
the morning after the bar has been trashed

NOTES

A … indicates a pause.

A / indicates the beginning of the next line, an interruption in speech.

for sean and lucky.

for the places i've danced with reckless abandon.
for the people who have spun me across a floor.
and as much as i tried for it not to be,
for florida.

and for you.
yes, you.
if you're reading this,
it's for you.

my boots are laced for you.

ONE

(It should be visible before it even begins.)

(The bar
wrecked,
bottles smashed, surfaces smudged.
It's littered with smashed glass.)

*(*MINNOW, CAT, *and* AUDRA
trying to clean but not knowing where to start.
Frozen in that paradox of disbelief but also complete belief.)

(They look at each other.
In a split second:)

(Loud music.
It should be what someone might describe as "angry" when really, it's joyful.)

(A small moment of what it is like in an opening shift.
They turn over three barstools [none of them match],
They count cash,
They take out three shot glasses [they don't match either]
They go to clear a space to put their shot glasses down.
They knock into wreckage.)

(Wreckage)

(Right)

(They come back to the present.)

(A deep breath.
We are here now.
All together,
here.)

TWO

MINNOW:
Check in?

CAT:
You want a check in right now?

MINNOW:
Yeah, I really need one.

AUDRA:
Fair.

MINNOW:
Dearly beloved.

*(*MINNOW *waits.*
MINNOW *and* AUDRA *look to* CAT.
It's clearly CAT*'s turn.)*

CAT:
Queerly beloved.

MINNOW:
We are gathered here today.
(She pours three shots.)

CAT:
To get through this thing called life.

*(*AUDRA *pours another shot.)*

AUDRA:
But first, to get through this shift.
(She places the shot somewhere holy quite carefully.)

CAT:
I've got a check-in.

*(*MINNOW *slides a shot to* CAT.*)*

CAT:
Ready to put 2016 to bed.
Like, tuck it in
and whisper it sweet nothings.

That's what I want to do.
(They take the shot.)

AUDRA:
I've got a check-in.

*(*MINNOW *slides a shot to* AUDRA.*)*

AUDRA:
I thought,
I just thought maybe
We could have been spared
I thought this place could be spared from something like this.

MINNOW:
Passed over.

CAT:
Like some Moses shit.
Old testament passed over.

AUDRA:
No.
Like some real world
"hate-has-no-predictability and maybe we got lucky" shit.
Apparently not.
(She takes the shot.)

MINNOW:
I got a check-in.
(She brings a shot closer to herself.)
Pulled
between the comfort of you two
and the discomfort of this place.
and still, somehow
the comfort of this place.
That's what it feels like.

AUDRA:
How long have you been in here alone?

MINNOW:
Not long.
It took the cops a while to get a hold of me.
They kept trying to contact / Maggie.

CAT:
Maggie.

MINNOW:
And I texted you both as I was walking up
So however long it took for you two to get here.

AUDRA:
What did they say?

MINNOW:
There's no sign of forced entry.

CAT:
Shit.

AUDRA:
I locked the back, I swear /
I mean I think I locked the back.

MINNOW:
No, no, I believe you.
And I know I locked the front.
And we all know those locks are shitty, they could have been picked just as easily.
It's no ones fault.

CAT:
What about our security footage?

MINNOW:
The police get to review it once the report is filed.
See if there's anything on it.

AUDRA:
God, how did we get here.

MINNOW:
And where the hell do we go now.

CAT:
What did Maggie have to say about all of this?

*(*MINNOW *takes her shot.)*

MINNOW:
We can't reach her.
She's still / out of…

CAT:
In the fucking Caribbean.
Right.
Great time to go on a vacation you told / no one about.

MINNOW:
It's fine.
We don't need her.
We have the clear to act as we see fit.
As I see fit.
Until Maggie comes back or until she gets cell reception to say otherwise,
It's my call.
She left me in charge when she / decided to

CAT:
Ghosted.
When she ghosted.
I'm not being kind to her,
You can, but I won't.

AUDRA:
Minnow, what can I get you?

MINNOW:
It's enough that you're here.

*(*AUDRA *pours a glass of water anyways.*
In fact, she pours water for everyone.)

CAT:
We should pile the wreckage,
Offer it up as a gift.
A middle-finger gift.

MINNOW:
We'll save what we can and throw out the rest.

AUDRA:
I can't get myself to do it, Minnow.
Every time I walk towards the glass, my body just stops.

MINNOW:
I know.

CAT:
Same.

AUDRA:
Someone remind me what it is when it's good.

CAT:
Eleven PM.

MINNOW:
Ha.

CAT:
No, literally, it's the best time.

MINNOW:
The low chatter starts to pick up into the steady hum of voices.

CAT:
More bodies in the space, more energy bouncing off each other.

(AUDRA picks up a larger chunk of mirror.)

AUDRA:
The sound of glasses clinking, the music getting perceptibly louder.

CAT:
That stupid light that's always flickering decides to work.

MINNOW:
I fixed it two nights ago.

*(*AUDRA *bounces light off of the shard of mirror.*
CAT *starts to collect trash.)*

CAT:
Ugh, YES there was such a good glow across the faces last night.

*(*AUDRA *bounces light onto* MINNOW.*)*

AUDRA:
You were trying to fix the dishwasher when I came in.

MINNOW:
I didn't want to hand wash glasses all night.

CAT:
I kept saying this is why we should switch to plastic cups.
Just own the fact that The Beacon is a plastic cup establishment.
We shouldn't try to be something we are not.

*(*MINNOW *starts to sweep.*
AUDRA *takes a look at herself for a moment.*
Then she throws the shard of mirror into a trash can.
The three of them slow to a stop.
A moment.)

AUDRA:
Keep going?

CAT/MINNOW/AUDRA: Keep going.

(We blink and we're in it. 11PM. It's alive and it's beautiful.)

THREE

(The top of the night clips along. They're putting things in the places they like for their shift.)

AUDRA:
Oooh, it's young in here tonight.
You didn't tell me Friday nights are this young.

MINNOW:
You're young, babycakes.

AUDRA:
No!
They're way younger than me!

CAT:
Which one is the friend who swears they're not gay?

MINNOW:
That's so mean.

CAT:
I know the type because I was the type.
I can be mean because I'm mostly just dragging myself, okay?

(All three crack open their energy drink of choice.
CAT *is looking at someone—or some ones—in the crowd.)*

AUDRA:
Stop throwing glances at the babies.
They're so scared.
They don't know the look across the room yet.

CAT:
And how else are they going to learn?

AUDRA:
You're going to intimidate them.

CAT:
Good.
It's not like I'm gonna / bite.

MINNOW:
Not unless someone / asks.

CAT:
Do you remember the first person to give you the look across a bar?
Like the first person to do it where you were like
Uh oh, maybe I want this.

MINNOW:
Hell yeah.
And I was scared out of my mind.

AUDRA:
You?
Scared?

MINNOW:
Quaking in my Docs.

CAT:
Of course you owned Docs.

AUDRA:
(To CAT*)* You're wearing Docs, bitch.

(This is true.)

MINNOW:
She had broad shoulders.

CAT:
Mmm.

AUDRA:
Is that what does it for you?
Broad shoulders?

MINNOW:
Do you remember the first person to own themselves so well,
They taught you there was more than one way to be?

AUDRA:
I get it.

MINNOW:
You're not sure if you're attracted to them
Or if you just want to be them?

CAT:
Both, usually.

*(*MINNOW *taps her own shoulders.)*

MINNOW:
Broad shoulders.
It was like.
Oh there I am.
Oh there you are.

CAT:
The light in me sees the light in you of it all, yeah.

*(*AUDRA *yawns.)*

CAT:
Don't fall asleep!
It's not even witching hour yet.

*(*AUDRA *flips* CAT *the bird, still mid-yawn.)*

CAT:
Too early for yawns.

AUDRA:
Sorry.
It's been a long day.

CAT:
Long week, friend.

AUDRA:
Long year and there's still two months to go.

(They clink shot glasses.)

CAT:
If the world ends on election night,
Maybe I'll get a full eight hours sleep.

AUDRA:
It's not even the election.
It's just like
Raise other people's kids in the day.
Watch adults become babies at night.

CAT:
Who'd you have to babysit today?

AUDRA:
Correction, who pushed me to the edge until I quit today.

CAT:
Woooooooah.

MINNOW:
Oh, shit.

AUDRA:
That's why I picked up the last-minute cover.

(CAT and MINNOW both separately pour AUDRA a shot and put them down in front of her.)

CAT/MINNOW: Congrats.

(AUDRA pushes the shots away.)

AUDRA:
I don't know.
With the way these finances are looking, I'm going to have to find another kid to watch.

MINNOW:
You might not need to.
Just wait and see what late night tips look like
Friday nights are a different animal than Sunday brunch.

CAT:
What finally did you in?

AUDRA:
Agnes has had a fever for a week straight.

No other symptoms,
Just a fever.
She just spent all day cheeks pressed against the kitchen tiles,
tearing holes in the lace on her dress and crying.
It's like she knows that she should be burning right now.
Her two-year-old body is burning
and who am I to tell her that she's wrong?
Like all this shit is metaphorically on fire.
But I looked at her today and I was like,
I'm on fire too.
I can't help you.

CAT:
Woof.

(A moment)

AUDRA:
Shit, I think we got high school kids.
Do they look like high school kids to you?

MINNOW:
Almost certainly.
Fuck.

CAT:
Hold on, I got it.
I'll card them again when they order.
I want to see the craftsmanship on their fakes.

*(*AUDRA *stifles another yawn.)*

MINNOW:
Let me know if you need some coffee.
I stashed a cup from King Corona under here.
We can always send one of us out to get more.

AUDRA:
What about "No Outside Drinks In The Bar"?

MINNOW:
It's Maggie's rule, not mine
And she's snorkeling off Turks and Caicos right now.
She's never going to find out.

*(*MINNOW *slides a coffee cup towards* AUDRA.*)*

MINNOW:
One day I'll own this place.
I'll buy it out from under her.
Or she will die and leave it to me.
She wouldn't curse anyone else with this place in her will.
And when that happens we will also serve café
And make a killing and the joke will be on her
But, until then.

AUDRA:
Contraband coffee from down the street.

MINNOW:
I hope she felt that sip all the way in the Caribbean.

*(*AUDRA *slides the cup back.*
MINNOW *tucks it away safely.*
CAT *comes back.)*

CAT:
Fuckin' high school kids trying to order a rum and coke.
I asked them if they had preference on rum and they said
"Jack Daniel's is fine"
Like
Fuck outta here.
Like can't you just say "no preference"?
Better yet, can't you just say "Jack and coke" if the only thing you know is Jack?

AUDRA:
What'd you pour?

CAT:
Coke and the infused simple syrup.
Real fancy and fast so they couldn't tell.
I hope their pediatric dentist thanks me for their cavities.
They're almost certainly children, but the IDs look good.

MINNOW:
How do high school kids even get passable fake IDs?
I never got a good fake in high school.

AUDRA:
They wire gobs of money to strangers from the internet.
It's all really sketchy.

CAT:
It's so rich that I can't get an ID without gender on it
But these fucks can say they're anyone in the world.

MINNOW:
These fucks are also drinking raw sugar at this point.

AUDRA:
Babies.

MINNOW:
It's early.
They'll filter out before it gets really raucous in here.
No stamina.

*(*CAT *grabs some supplies from under the bar.)*

CAT:
I gotta go clean off the side bar again.
I think they're using both bar tops for the first performance.
And if someone slips on condensation from the / youth—

MINNOW:
Hold up.
Check in.

CAT:
It's a bit late for a check in, don't you think?

*(*MINNOW *pours another shot to join Audra's rejected celebration shots.*
They look to one another.)

MINNOW:
Dearly beloved,

CAT:
Queerly beloved,

MINNOW:
We are gathered here today—

CAT:
To get through this Friday night shift.

AUDRA:
Pour one out for Prince.

MINNOW:
There's already one from last night.

AUDRA:
You're going to leave Prince a stale drink?
A STALE OFFERING?

MINNOW:
Oh my god, okay.

*(*CAT *grabs the shot from Minnow's hand.*
They literally pour a shot for Prince.
It's placed somewhere sacred.
MINNOW *pours another shot while she speaks.)*

MINNOW:
Okay, real fast
And we can go back to pouring cavity cocktails.

CAT:
Alright
We've got drag every hour on the hour
Or, you know,
When it happens.
Please be extra kind, we've got Orlando queens in the house.
June was not that long ago, I do not know how rattled everyone is,
And I'm glad they feel ready and willing and able to perform tonight.

MINNOW:
You gonna jump in, too?

CAT:
Absolutely not.

MINNOW:
C'mon Cat.
Everyone loved it.
And Audra didn't get to see it.

CAT:
No, tonight I'm here to honor art.
Not do my own.
That's what I got.
Audra, check in.

AUDRA:
We are done with Halloween specials
Thank god
Because orange jello shots taste heinous
And Halloween is a trash holiday

*(*CAT *begins to protest—)*

AUDRA:
I will not be convinced otherwise
We are back to normal drinks,
but Cat and I are maybe fucking around with new

citrus cocktails.
Actual citrus, not that fake orange shit.

CAT:
Maybe a temperance drink?

MINNOW:
Ooooh, a little mocktail moment?

CAT:
Yeah, like Blood Orange.

AUDRA:
With like soda and agave
And lime and mint.

CAT:
Oh my god, you're an artist.

AUDRA:
Right?
Wouldn't that taste good?

MINNOW:
To have year-round?

AUDRA:
Yes.
Unless Maggie nixes.

MINNOW:
Well, I don't see her.

AUDRA:
Me either.

MINNOW:
And on my front, Clark and Megh are front door from here on out.
We've got Ariel in the DJ booth all night.
She's got some new tracks she made with her sister in Havana
And she's dropping them at midnight so please listen and let people know

I did hear one already and it is straight fire and hella Cubana so you know I'm already here for it.
…
Anything else business?

(Everyone shakes their heads.)

MINNOW:
Personal?
It can be flash.
Anything we gotta know?

AUDRA:
Underslept but here.

MINNOW:
Heard.
Still haven't heard from Maggie,
But we're making the bar work anyways.

AUDRA:
And your heart?

MINNOW:
Still haven't heard from Maggie,
But I'm hearing a heartbeat anyways.
Gotta be good enough for now.
Cat?

CAT:
Working on making it through the first week of November.

*(*CAT *looks over to the high school kids.)*

AUDRA:
Look at them.
Doing that "I'm so drunk" thing.

CAT:
Beautiful idiots.

AUDRA:
They just look so free.

CAT:
...
They don't know any better yet.

MINNOW:
Hey.
I'm glad it's us tonight.
This feels like the dream team.

*(They all take their shots.
We shift back to the day after.)*

FOUR

MINNOW:
God what a nightmare.

AUDRA:
Do you think Maggie is going to fire us?
Like is she going to / blame us.

CAT:
No. This wasn't our fault.
It could be someone who sits here comfortably
Who just carefully holds their rage in the palm of their hands.
Maggie gets that.
You remember the first Thanksgiving we had here, Minnow?

AUDRA:
You guys used to host Thanksgiving here?

MINNOW:
Maggie did.
It started small, just some bartenders with no place to go.
And then it got too big
We had to move it from her place upstairs down to the bar.

CAT:
She invited everyone who didn't have a place to go.
Not just people who worked here but people who came here, too.
And this was back when it was a real shitshow
And the bar didn't really have a visible identity then
And it turned out one of the regulars didn't realize he was coming to a gay bar,
Especially / one owned and operated by a woman.

AUDRA:
Ah.

MINNOW:
He called her a faggot
and Maggie said I prefer dyke and then threw mashed potatoes at him.
and then physically threw him out on the street.

CAT:
She was so proud of herself.
She kept saying

CAT/MINNOW:
FLORIDA MAN TOSSED OUT OF BAR COVERED IN MASHED POTATOES.

AUDRA:
Well, it's impossible to not realize you've walked into a gay bar now.

CAT:
Yeah, for better and worse, apparently.

(A moment.
MINNOW *smirks.)*

MINNOW:
Do you remember how dry that fucking turkey always was?

CAT:
It was like chewing on wood chips.

MINNOW:
There was other food too.
Thankfully.

CAT:
Yeah but only because people brought like
Generic puffy Cheetos and pizza.

AUDRA:
Why did Maggie stop hosting Thanksgiving?

CAT:
Maggie said it was because the bar lost too much money in liquor one year.

MINNOW:
It was really because I'd moved my stuff out of Maggie's that Halloween.

AUDRA:
You lived with Maggie?

MINNOW:
We tried not to let anyone know.

CAT:
I knew.
We all knew.

MINNOW:
I know.
Everyone knew the whole time.
I don't know why we thought it was a secret.

CAT:
With both of you going upstairs to Maggie's after closing?

MINNOW:
I thought I was sneaky when I was twenty-four, okay?

AUDRA:
I didn't realize you and Maggie were ever a real thing.
Instead of…

MINNOW:
The bullshit we've been doing?
Yeah.
Well.
She used to be fun.

CAT:
You gotta realize, Audra,
she used to be around.

MINNOW:
And she used to throw a mean right hook in the face of some homophobic motherfuckers,
that's for sure.

AUDRA:
But would she close down the bar, do you think?
Our weeknights are slow and now this…

MINNOW:
Nah, that's how it works.
Some nights are slow, some nights are over capacity.

*(*MINNOW *begins to sweep debris into a trash bag.*
CAT *throws a warning glance at* AUDRA.*)*

AUDRA:
But when's the last time / we've even seen her?

MINNOW:
We're not losing our jobs.
We aren't closing down.
We aren't giving up.

AUDRA:
You aren't giving up, but Maggie / might.

MINNOW:
What do you / want to do?

AUDRA:
I'm allowed to not know what I want to do right now.
I just want to be prepared.

MINNOW:
Okay.

AUDRA:
I don't know what I want to do.
I don't know what I want Maggie to do.
Okay?

MINNOW:
Okay.

AUDRA:
Okay.

MINNOW:
Okay.

AUDRA:
I didn't mean to bring up Maggie losing hope in us.

MINNOW:
She doesn't give up hope in us.
Just me.

CAT:
I just want to point out that this line of conversation never leads you down a good path, Minnow.

MINNOW:
No, it's different this time, because I'm the one she's gonna blame for this.
If we close, she's going to make it my fault.
She gave me this fucked up little test and I failed it.

CAT:
Did you smash the glass?

MINNOW:
No.

CAT:
Then you didn't fail anything.
Or anyone.
Not yourself.

Not either of us.
Not anyone who was in here last night having the time of their lives.

AUDRA:
Don't you think that's the most twisted part.
It was a really good night.

CAT:
A really good night.

MINNOW:
Ariel's newest tracks.

CAT:
Yeah
Midnight.

MINNOW:
Oh my god, don't look at me like that.

CAT:
From what I remember, you were counting down the minutes.

AUDRA:
Loudly.

CAT:
And then the seconds
Like it was New Year's Eve.

(Time begins to blur.
MINNOW *checks her phone.)*

MINNOW:
Oh my god, it's almost time.

AUDRA:
I know.

MINNOW:
Is Ariel ready?
ARIEL ARE YOU READY?
TEN

AUDRA
Oh my god.

NINE
EIGHT
SEVEN
SIX
FIVE
FOUR
THREE
TWO

This track better be good.

CAT:
And then—

*(We linger in that second before.
The tension is beautiful.)*

CAT:
You got wild, babe.

*(The new track floods the space.
Let's go.)*

FIVE

MINNOW:
MIDNIGHT! MIDNIGHT! MIDNIGHT!

(Pop a bottle)

MINNOW:
Are you *hearing this genius right now?*
Oh my god all Cuban music is dance music.
Why aren't you dancing?

CAT:
Is this going to end with you dancing on the bar with a customer again?

MINNOW:
Okay, but did it bring the cash tips up?

CAT:
Fair.

MINNOW:
Oh my god, do you hear it.
The shells.
Ariel put the sound of the shells in.
The way she hears the world is unreal.
Ariel!! Yes!!
Why is no one else appreciating this.
Do you see anyone out there who is like
As mindblown as I am?

AUDRA:
Why? Are you looking tonight, Minnow?

MINNOW:
I'm not *not* looking.
Hey!
I'm just keeping my eyes open.

CAT:
She's not not *looking.*

AUDRA:
For the perfect person who doesn't exist?

MINNOW:
I don't think I'm being unreasonable!

AUDRA:
If you keep saying you only want *one thing* in a new partner
And that *one thing* changes every day

MINNOW:
It doesn't change every day.

AUDRA:
Every week, then.

CAT:
Last week it was that they had to cook like a Michelin chef.

MINNOW:
I didn't say / *Michelin chef.*

AUDRA:
Two Sundays ago, it was that they had to play an instrument.

MINNOW:
Dexterity / come on.

CAT:
Yesterday you told me it would be nice if they speak Spanish.

MINNOW:
They don't need to be *fluent*.
but Maggie didn't speak any Spanish and I want someone to know that side / of me.

AUDRA:
And what'll it be tomorrow?

MINNOW:
It would be nice if they could keep plants alive.

*(*AUDRA *cackles.)*

AUDRA:
What / else.

CAT:
You are enabling / her.

AUDRA:
This is my favorite pastime,
Don't deprive me.

MINNOW:
Maybe if they were a Libra.

CAT:
A Libra?!

MINNOW:
What's wrong with a Libra?

CAT:
You think you'll voluntarily give up the spotlight like that?

MINNOW:
We'll just take turns complimenting each other.
Tonight, though,
Tonight it's enough if they really understand this beat.

(CAT has been handed a cigar by someone in the club.)

CAT:
You want a puff?
Juana brought it in.
She says it's a real Cubano and I trust her.

AUDRA:
You literally cannot smoke that in here.

CAT:
I'll teach you how to blow smoke rings.

AUDRA:
You don't know how to blow smoke rings.

CAT:
I do, too.

AUDRA:
Since when.

CAT:
Years.
Minnow taught me.

AUDRA:
Who taught you?

MINNOW:
Lira.

(CAT starts to unwrap the cigar.)

CAT:
Audra, don't get her started.

MINNOW:
Oh, come on.
This is the point in the night where someone's usually leaning over the bar going
Who's Lira?
And no one is taking the bait tonight, Cat!
Help a Gemini out!

*(*CAT *laughs.*
It's all very fun.)

CAT:
I'm not going to flirt with you for sport.

AUDRA:
...
Who's Lira?

CAT:
Audra!
Oh my god.

AUDRA:
It's fun!

CAT:
Get your / popcorn.

(This is to AUDRA*,*
Mostly, at first
But we watch MINNOW *search the not-seen crowd for someone to flirt with.*
Someone to entertain.)

MINNOW:
When I was growing up
When my dad wasn't home.
Edelira would come drink café.
Mami would let us blast Celia Cruz
and La Lupe
and Gloria Estefan

*a volumen *prendido**
God, I used to love when Lira would come over.

CAT:
Do you know if we have a guillotine for this or should I just use a sharp knife?

AUDRA:
Are you really going to smoke that in here?

*(*MINNOW *spins* AUDRA *around to dance to grab her attention back.)*

MINNOW:
Mami would look at me and go
"Watch the pros"
And they would glide together
My mother leading but they were
one being.
Un solo cuerpo, Minnow. *(One body)*
That's how you have to dance
Lira taught me how to count to the beat
And the kitchen would be a dance floor
And we'd throw the windows wide open
For anyone who wanted to listen

*(*MINNOW *spins around* AUDRA.
She finds someone at the bar who has been watching.
Someone listening.
Someone cute who might not need a translator.)

MINNOW:
I remember how red my father flushed
when I asked
Why do you lead Mami but Mami leads Lira
That's when I learned
Mami y Lira no eran simplemente amigas.
(And that's when I learned that Mom and Lira weren't just friends.)

*(*MINNOW *should know who is in the room with her.*
Really with her.
And this is for them.
But mostly for her)

MINNOW:
Medianoche es de Mami y Lira
(Midnight is for Mom and Lira)
Las tortilleras en formación y las bollos pequeñas
(Baby queers part the way for the OG dykes.)
Las hijas de las hijas
(The daughters of the daughters of the women)
que rollaban cigarrillos por allá
(who rolled cigarettes on the corner)
Y boquean cuando ven como bailan las muchachas
(And they gasp at how smooth the women dance)
Como si fueran un solo cuerpo
(Like they are all one body)
Y detrás del bar
(And from behind the bar—)
Fuck it—
(She climbs on top of the bar.)
Y encima del bar
(And from atop the bar)
I can steal a few moments to dance.

CAT:
Audra, we should pick up the slack because
Minnow
is dancing and not doing her job.

*(*MINNOW *holds up her middle finger and keeps dancing.)*

AUDRA:
I think she caught someone.

CAT:
Who'd you catch?

MINNOW:
Esta noche, estoy enamorada de mi misma
(Tonight, I'm in love with myself)

CAT:
I know you love yourself.
That's not what I asked!

*(*MINNOW *laughs.)*

AUDRA:
That's kind of a fucked up story.
with her mom and dad.
She's just put a good twist on it.

CAT:
The twist being her mom got Lira
And they got to grow old being cute old Cuban lesbians together?
It's a good twist.

AUDRA:
But the part she isn't saying
The part after her dad found out
What happened?

CAT:
Ask her yourself.

*(*MINNOW *hops down off the bar.)*

CAT:
How was the view up there, Minnow?

MINNOW:
Breathtaking.
I hope when I'm sixty, I'm still out dancing past midnight.
On the tops of bars.
Seventy, eighty even.
Someone young and cute will have to boost me up.

AUDRA:
What if Maggie catches you doing it first.

MINNOW:
Maggie's the first person I ever saw dancing on this bar.

AUDRA:
I call / bullshit.

MINNOW:
Deadass.
...
Look at the girl at the end of the bar.
I'm going to see if she needs anything.

AUDRA:
I knew it. I knew you caught someone.

MINNOW:
Be right back.

CAT:
Great,
now I'm picking up the slack because
Minnow
is *flirting*
and not *doing her job.*

MINNOW:
Flirting is most of the job, queen.

*(*CAT *ponders.)*

CAT:
...
Something is off.

AUDRA:
Nope.

CAT:
You can't bullshit a witch at midnight.

There's something going on.
Spit it out.

AUDRA:
Long day.
I told you.

CAT:
Long week.

AUDRA:
Long crushing / history of doing the hustle

CAT:
history of doing the hustle
I feel you.

(AUDRA cleans a glass.
Obsessively.
MINNOW *returns to pour a pint of beer.)*

MINNOW:
You trying to rub a hole through the glass?

AUDRA:
The dishwasher is fucked, okay!

CAT:
Woah.

MINNOW:
Is this about something / not-bar-related?

AUDRA:
No.

MINNOW:
Because we can talk about whatever it is you need to / talk about.

AUDRA:
No, Minnow.
Just like, go back to flirting with girls at the bar.
I'm fine.

(MINNOW *grabs the glass from* AUDRA.
She puts it where it belongs.
She walks away.)

CAT:
Do you need some time alone?
Maybe just like, cut a fuckton of lime slices or something.

AUDRA:
Really, I'm okay.

(They grab a glass for AUDRA.*)*

CAT:
At least take a drink—

AUDRA:
I've had a drink tonight, okay?
I don't need to loosen up.

CAT:
Of water.
A drink *of water.*
...
Look.
She'll tell you if you just ask her.
She'll tell you all about the fights and the not-divorce
and how it stopped her from coming out to her dad for years
But she'll also tell you about watching her mom and Lira be in love
real love
joyful love
And how Lira became the second parent she needed
And I think
right now
for so many reasons, she has to lean into the joy.
(They nudge the water closer.)
(They slip back to the other side of the bar.)

There's a lot of shit going on right now,
And always,
And to look at the shit is necessary
Right?
To not escape into some fantasy land of everything is okay
When it's not.
But to look at the joy is harder,
To mine it out, to find it hiding
To practice seeing through the absolute hell of it
As a survival tactic.
To say it's just as bad as I think it is
And I'm still breathing
And I'm still breathing for this
To know what keeps you tethered to it all.
And when the joy is hard to find,
When you grasp it,
Even for a moment,
I think we have to lean in full tilt.
Just to try to and see what you learn from it?
Or not even for a point
To remind yourself that you can feel joy still.
To just live in the joy for as long as you can.
(They nudge the water closer.
They slip back to the other side of the bar.)
Maybe you should dance on the bar for a while.
The tip jar might thank you,
And your nervous system might thank you too.

(We shift back to the day after.)

SIX

*(*CAT, *on the other side of the bar, cleaning up shards of glass.)*

MINNOW:
I'll tell you.

*(*MINNOW *grabs a broom and begins sweeping.)*

AUDRA:
We don't have to get into it, Minnow.
Not if you don't want to.

MINNOW:
No, I want to explain it to you I want you to have some context.
Because you're right.
There were fights,
lots of fights and a not-divorce
but there was love.
Real love.
My mother chose love.
And Lira became a third parent.
And yes, it fucked up my relationship with my dad
And it made things complicated when my mother died
because technically
by law, things went to my father
But even that brought him back to me
And we were doing so well lately,
We were really patching things,
and he called me yesterday before my shift,
He called me just to check in on me,
He knows I love a check in,
But he told me that he
is voting red
And
I didn't have it in me to try and talk him out of it
And deep down, I think I knew that's how he was going to vote anyways
And so I just hung up on him.
And I came in here for the night.
And
All I wanted to do was talk to Maggie about it.

CAT:
Minnow.

MINNOW:
No, don't Minnow me.
She was my person for a long time, you know.
She's been here for me through a lot of rough shit.

CAT:
We can be here for you through a lot of rough shit.

MINNOW:
But she has the history of it.
And I just came in here and it was like there was this giant, empty space without her.
And that's when Cat told me that Ariel had new music
And I felt it
All of me
And it felt like a sign from my mother.
It felt like she was giving me time to be me.
Every single facet of me.
Of us, really.
Of the parts of her she couldn't help but give to me.
The parts of me I never got the chance to fully tell her
But that she probably knew without me saying it.
Completely, wholly, all of me.
And it was really beautiful up here.
I felt really beautiful.

AUDRA:
Thank you.
I didn't know.
That you were carrying all of that last night.

MINNOW:
We don't ever know
We don't know what people are going through.
I'm sure you had shit last night I didn't know about and
I just think
I just wish
Sometimes I just wish we all gave each other a little

more
I don't know.
...
Guys, I don't know if Maggie's coming back.

CAT:
She can't stay on a cruise ship forever.

MINNOW:
Most of her stuff is gone.
Upstairs?
I mean, her stuff is still here but
All the things she cared about
All the little things that made it her place,
They're gone.

CAT:
That's cowardly as fuck.

MINNOW:
Is it?
She always said she would leave
She never had any problem putting her body first.

AUDRA:
...
So, we're largely
Alone.

MINNOW:
I feel like I woke up one day and suddenly I was the adult in the room
And I have no idea how I got here.
I mean, I get it—
I'm the one who stayed when my mother got sick
I'm the one who stayed to make sure Lira was take care of
And it's not as simple for me as just up and leaving, you know?
I don't want to leave
My life is here

It's not perfect, but it's here.
I kissed a girl for the first time in the Centro Ybor Muvico for fuck's sake.
José Martí Park is literally Cuban territory.
I know people here, people know me.
It's all here.
But it's getting harder to be here.
I can zip up my black jeans
And wing my eyeliner
And I can lace up my combat boots as tight as they will go
I just keep getting up every morning and putting on my armor
Like every other day for the past ten years
But it's not working anymore.
What do I do when it stops working completely?
...
I've got to figure out how to fix my armor
Because it's not just about me anymore.
And it probably never was.

*(*MINNOW *cleans.*
CAT *and* AUDRA *watch her clean.*
No one is certain what to say.
A deep breath, and then)

AUDRA:
One am.

(We shift.)

SEVEN

*(*CAT *is making a very complicated drink.*
There's an egg white involved.)

AUDRA:
Are you calling me a bitch right now?

CAT:
I'm saying Minnow looks pretty happy right now
and you look pretty miserable.
Wait
Now that I think about it,
Yes
I am saying that.

*(*AUDRA *glares at* CAT.*)*

CAT:
You know I call you out because I love you.

(The glare continues.)

CAT:
Your glares won't get you anywhere.
You know that about me.
I'm not one of your toddlers.

AUDRA:
I was hoping you'd be Switzerland in this moment.

CAT:
This is as Switzerland as I get, you know that.

AUDRA:
What are we even making right now?

*(*CAT *begins to vigorously shake the shaker.)*

CAT:
Have you been paying attention?

AUDRA:
No, you've been calling me a bitch.

CAT:
A Ramos Gin Fizz.

*(*CAT *opens the shaker and add ice.*
They continue to shake.)

AUDRA:
Let me do that.

CAT:
You gotta do it really hard.

AUDRA:
I got it.

(CAT hands over the shaker.
AUDRA shakes.)

CAT:
Harder than that.
It's not your run-of-the-mill Gin Fizz.
It's usually a Mardi Gras drink,
We're still manifesting Tulane, right?

AUDRA:
Sure, with all the money I've got to go to med school / right now.

CAT:
Do you not understand manifesting.

AUDRA:
Yes.
Okay.
Tulane.

CAT:
And if you're working through med school
I want you to be somewhere nice
Somewhere that regularly has egg white drinks.

(CAT pulls down a Collins glass.
AUDRA opens the shaker
Then she pours the drink in.)

AUDRA:
That looks really gross.

(CAT holds the drink up.)

CAT:
Didn't shake it hard enough so the egg didn't foam it up right.

You want it to look like its mostly foam
You want a really, frothy, head.

*(*AUDRA *flicks soda water at* CAT.
CAT *grabs a lemon slice.)*

AUDRA:
Put that down.
Teach me again.

*(*CAT *puts the lemon slice in their mouth like it's candy.)*

AUDRA:
Teach me again.

CAT:
You're distracted.

AUDRA:
Nothing's fucking wrong.

CAT:
Something's wrong.

AUDRA:
I literally quit a job today?

CAT:
Yeah and I feel that all over your throat chakra
But there's something else, too.

AUDRA:
You're not going to let this go, are you?

CAT:
It's like a cloud around you.
Just let it all out.
No one's fucking listening right now.

AUDRA:
My vag is broken.

CAT:
I told you
All that junk / builds up if they don't wash right.

AUDRA:
No. No. No. No.

CAT:
This is why I am on a dick hiatus.
Literal and figurative

AUDRA:
But I want to sometimes
Not figurative dicks.
Never a figurative dick.
But literal ones, kind of.
Depending on whose.

CAT:
You sound so convincing right now.

AUDRA:
I mean
No
No one wants to
Not like a hundred percent of the time
No one's ever like
You know what's not weird?
Genitalia
Because we aren't conditioned to believe it's not weird
But it's because it's weird sometimes
That it works
It's like
let me put my weird near your weird
or
in your weird
or
on your weird
and like,
feel good
you know?

CAT:
Don't make me reconsider my hiatus like this.

AUDRA:
Because bodies are so weird
and I love them because they're weird
And sometimes that person that I want to explore weird with
Has a dick
And I remember when dicks didn't feel like
getting a pap smear with a serrated knife.

CAT:
Make us some Gin Fizzes and explain.

(CAT *grabs eggs from a fridge and puts them in front of* AUDRA.)

AUDRA:
Repeat it again for me?

CAT:
2 Gin
½ Heavy cream
½ Lemon juice
½ Lime juice
¾ simple syrup
egg white
little bit of orange blossom water

AUDRA:
Orange blossom water?

CAT:
Yeah.
It's a fancy ass drink.
Don't fuck it up again.

(*They put the orange blossom water in front of* AUDRA.)

CAT:
You don't have to dry shake if you only use six ice cubes.

AUDRA:
There's no way that recipe will work.

CAT:
It works.
Now spill. What's this vulvic issue.
Vulvic?
Vulvaic.

AUDRA:
Gyneco/logical.

CAT:
Nah, I like / vulvic better.

AUDRA:
It's like
broken.

CAT:
Like UTI broken?
Because that's uterine, med school.

AUDRA:
Fuck you,
I know that's uterine.
My pelvic floor muscles are…

(CAT begins to separate two egg whites from their yolks.)

AUDRA:
My pelvic floor muscles are seemingly continuously clenched.
It's apparently a problem that could have been around for years.
But I wouldn't know
Because there hasn't been much

CAT:
Penetration

AUDRA:
Yeah.

CAT:
Say the word I dare you.

AUDRA:
Not a time to joke, Cat.

CAT:
Audra
It is kind of funny, isn't it?

AUDRA:
Sometimes.
Sometimes, it is a little funny.

CAT:
How long has it been since you slept with someone that wasn't queer?

AUDRA:
Five / years

CAT:
Five years and now
Your pelvic floor muscles are confused

(AUDRA *slams the shaker down.)*

AUDRA:
Don't go there, Cat.
I'm warning you.

CAT:
Oh, Audra, it's mostly / a joke—

(AUDRA *drops the egg whites into the shaker.)*

AUDRA:
It's a bad joke and I told you that from the beginning.
But you latched onto it, Cat.

CAT:
I think the straight cisgender man can be the butt of the joke, Audra.
He's gonna be okay.

(AUDRA *begins to vigorously shake the shaker.)*

AUDRA:
It's not just him that gets implicated in that joke!
No one was more surprised than about who I'm dating than me, okay.
No one gets to have more feelings about it than me.
Did I think his body would be the one to house his kind of soul? No.
But it is. So here I am.
And the kicker is I was just so scared to tell anyone about him.
Because I knew the comments were going to roll in.
I knew what I was going to hear
and my family was going to say shit like
does this mean you aren't gay anymore
as if every relationship I am in isn't a queer relationship
because I myself am queer
I'm queer as fuck
and I'm dating a straight man.
It happened without me even realizing it.
I just so desperately needed someone to look at me
And look through all the walls I put up
and say you don't scare me
and say I love you
Not in that friendship forever
let's buy matching necklaces way
or not even in the
thick as thieves kind of way
you know
I was looking for a partner
and I was worried that I would never find one
or
rather
that I was going to find one
but all of my walls will be built up so thick that I couldn't feel love
and if I can't feel the love

I won't believe the love
and I can't expect someone to brave the storm with me
if I cant even find it in me to say
thank you
and then he showed up
you know?
he just showed up
and it's more than thank you
it's more than you see me
it's so much him and so much me
and we are so beautifully fluid
and I feel like water when I'm around him
like I can seep into his skin.
I'm falling in love with him.
I love him so much I want to drown us both.

(A moment.
AUDRA *opens the shaker.*
Runs club soda over the middle section like before.
She pours into two Collins glasses.
CAT *takes a sip.)*

CAT:
It's good.

(AUDRA *sips.)*

AUDRA:
I don't know why it works.
But it really does.
It is really good.

CAT:
The drink or the man.

AUDRA:
Yes.
(They look out at the dance floor.
We shift back to the day after.)

EIGHT

MINNOW:
How do you fix it.
The clenching.

AUDRA:
Pelvic floor muscle exercises.
And like
This weird set of medical stretchers.

CAT:
That sounds archaic.

AUDRA:
Because it is.
It's not for fun.
They aren't like, toys
It's to like,
Reteach my muscles that
penetration
isn't a bad thing.
Oh, God.
I'm sorry.

MINNOW:
Why be sorry.

CAT:
You have nothing to be sorry about.

AUDRA:
Because it's just all coming out right now
And we just have so much to deal with already.
I just always toe the line between
let him in, it's okay, this is someone new and
I have known something like this before and it was horrible.
I'm—

CAT:
Don't say sorry.
It's fine, I promise.

AUDRA:
No, it's *not* fine, that's the whole problem.

CAT:
I just mean that we remember wreckage.
And it can take a while to remember what the safe before the wreckage even felt like.

MINNOW:
I'll fuck him up.
Whoever he / is.

AUDRA:
It happened in undergrad.
I don't even know where he is right now.
He graduated before me and moved back home.
He's out, like, living his life right now.
Somewhere in the panhandle,
He's far away from here.
I just don't want it to have this hold on me anymore.

CAT:
It might take a while to work its way out.
That's just human.

AUDRA:
How *much more time though.*
How long is this gonna take.
The whole thing feels like I'm just not working.
And I feel like I can't talk about it.
My actual reproductive system.
I feel like when something is wrong
It's not something I get to talk about.

CAT:
I'm always here to talk bluntly about anatomy.

AUDRA:
No, I know
I'm just not
Not always.

And I feel like when I talk about this,
I'm giving credence to the politicians who say shit like
Our bodies have ways of shutting that shit down
Because some people believe that.
I don't want anyone to think that's how it works.
I don't want anyone to think my superhuman pelvic muscles could like
Ward away invaders
That fuckery is how I got into this situation in the first place.
That if I didn't want it, he couldn't have done it.
And I walk around the world
Especially right now
And I think who around me thinks that way?

CAT:
Fuck `em.
You can't let them get to you.
You can't give them energy.

AUDRA:
But what does that mean, Cat?
Do you see how that's empty to me?
What does "you can't give them energy" even mean to me?
I need concrete steps.
And usually I can handle it.
Usually, I come in here
Even when I'm not working,
And we pull the blackout curtains closed
And I can feel the bass in the soles of my shoes
And I can at least think straight.

MINNOW:
There is something about walking into this room.
I always thought all would take to change someone's narrow-mindedness
would be to let them have a night in here.
Just let them watch from the sidelines.

AUDRA:
Really it might be the opposite.
Someone who comes in here narrow-minded
Just gets surrounded by all the things they hate.
And they just get more mad.
Don't you think?

CAT:
I think some people get more mad
but some people get more accepting.

MINNOW:
How do we know the difference?
How do we reach the people who just get more mad?

CAT:
Is it our job to?

MINNOW:
It is when they come in here and they tear it apart
When our things and
our bodies are at stake.

CAT:
I think all we can do is take care of our own
This community has so many good ghosts
And not a lot of living, breathing guides
We're doing all of this without a map of how to get
where we want to go.

MINNOW:
But Cat,
If we don't reach outside of us
We'll keep getting things like this.

*(They sit in it.
The muck.)*

AUDRA:
It's going to get worse.
Out there.
It's going to get worse.

MINNOW:
I know.

AUDRA:
I want to have a hand in the map-making.
If there's no map on where we want to go
We should write it together.
And I want to find it again.
The bass in the soles of my shoes.

MINNOW:
Okay.

CAT:
Okay.

AUDRA:
Okay.

MINNOW/CAT/AUDRA:

Two AM.

(A collective breath)

NINE

MINNOW:
Ariel's spinning something with a pulse.

AUDRA:
Like a heartbeat.

CAT:
Two am feels like everything is fluid

AUDRA:
Someone's tapping their fingers on the bar

MINNOW:
Someone's laughing
Really laughing

CAT:
Full body cackle

AUDRA:
Someone's hips are moving

CAT:
Nonverbal navigation of space

MINNOW:
Smooth

AUDRA:
Rhythmic

MINNOW:
One body

CAT:
Closer and closer

AUDRA:
Open

MINNOW:
Willing

AUDRA:
Heartbeat

CAT:
Sweaty

MINNOW:
The Beacon feels alive

AUDRA:
And we feel like a

CAT/MINNOW/AUDRA:
Well-oiled machine.
Glass
Ice
Right hand liquor
Left hand mixer

Look up
Witty banter
Smile
Garnish
Repeat

MINNOW:
The bachelorette party left!

(They cheer.)

CAT:
Glass
Ice
Right hand liquor
Left hand mixer
Look up
Witty banter
Smile
Garnish
Repeat.

*(*CAT *continues over.)*

AUDRA:
I can't even feel my feet anymore

MINNOW:
Standing for too long

AUDRA:
Kinda nice

*(*MINNOW *takes over for* CAT*'s repetition.)*

MINNOW:
Glass
Ice
Right hand liquor
Left hand mixer
Look up
Witty banter
Smile

Garnish
Repeat.

(MINNOW *continues over.)*

CAT:
Did you get the chance to see Brianna and Lily?

AUDRA:
They're back from the honeymoon?

CAT:
Tan as ever.
They'll come back up for another round.

(MINNOW *trades out with* AUDRA.)

MINNOW:
Comp their round!

AUDRA:
Glass
Ice
Right hand liquor
Left hand mixer
Look up
Witty banter
Smile
Garnish
Repeat.

CAT:
Juana is *still here*
Can you believe?

MINNOW:
Cuban hour, baby.
She got the music in her bones
And now she can't leave.

CAT:
Let me know if I should cut her off.

MINNOW:
I think we're good,
She's just sipping.
Oh shit.
The ice machines jammed.
(She starts to fix the ice machine.)
Ice.
Ice.
Ice.
Ice.
Ice.

(It continues under:)

AUDRA:
Gianni's here!

CAT:
I thought I heard their cackle!!
Already??

AUDRA:
It's been weeks!

CAT:
How do they look?

AUDRA:
See for yourself
They're showing their nipples to anyone and everyone

CAT:
Remember when Nico brought in pepperoni slices for everyone after his top surgery?

AUDRA:
The scars look gnarly

CAT:
They'll fade

AUDRA:
They look so happy

MINNOW:
Ice!

*(*AUDRA *collects all the empty glasses from the counter.)*

AUDRA:
Glass.
Glass.
Glass.
Glass.
Glass.

(It continues under.
CAT *clutches* MINNOW.*)*

CAT:
Oh my god, they're gonna do it

MINNOW:
They're gonna kiss?

CAT:
They're gonna kiss!

MINNOW:
THEY KISSED!

AUDRA:
Glasses!

CAT:
The baby queers kissed, Audra

AUDRA:
The world's longest foreplay
Oh my fucking god

CAT:
Shit we're out of mint
(They grab a mint plant stashed…somewhere.)
Garnish
Garnish
Garnish

Garnish
Garnish

(It continues.)

MINNOW:
I hate that I'm going to ask you this

AUDRA:
Do you need me to make a trash run?

MINNOW:
God, thank you for reading my mind

AUDRA:
It's fine
I need a breath of fresh air

MINNOW:
We're in a lull
Take your time

*(*AUDRA *leaves with trash.*
Together, CAT *and* MINNOW*:)*

CAT:	MINNOW:
Glass	Glass
Ice	Ice.
Right hand liquor	Right hand liquor
Left hand mixer	Left hand mixer
Look up	Look up
Witty banter	Witty banter
Smile	Smile
Garnish	Garnish
Repeat.	Repeat.
Glass	Glass
Ice	Ice
A breath	A breath
Lights go out	…
	Music goes out.

(Time slows.
Or they slow, to make sure they all hear each other's version.)

AUDRA:
From outside it sounds like a loud snap.
I think.
This is a part of Ariel's track.
But then the hair on my arms stand up.
What if it wasn't.

MINNOW:
And then the lights are back.

CAT:
Like nothing ever happened.

AUDRA:
And I remember thinking / how stupid I was to worry.

MINNOW:
How stupid I was to worry.

CAT:
The music comes back.

MINNOW:
I'm not back yet.

CAT:
I remember what happened
An hour away in a city I suddenly can't name.
All I see are Mouse ears.
I don't want it to be like this.
I don't want this room to become images of somewhere else.
This is different.
We're all different.
And yet in moments like this,
Through someone else's eyes,
We're made out to be all the same.
I want my eyes back.

MINNOW:
There's nothing in my gut.
Not a single helpful thought.
We went over this in June.
We made a plan in June.
But I didn't think in June,
What am I supposed to do
if I can't move.
Left hand gripping counter.
Spooked.

AUDRA:
Open the back door.

CAT:
Dread.

AUDRA:
Feet keep moving forward.

MINNOW:
Rehearse the emergency call
In my head
Over and over and over and over and

CAT:
Remember to breathe.

AUDRA:
Sticky floor under the soles of my shoes

MINNOW:
Audra grabs my hand.
And then Cat's.

(Time resumes.)

AUDRA:
I'm going to check in with Ariel.
Maybe something shorted on her end.

(AUDRA *leaves to find Ariel.*
CAT *is uncomfortable.*

They start to make a drink.
MINNOW *stops them.)*

MINNOW:
Are you okay?

CAT:
Spooked

MINNOW:
Yeah.

CAT:
Dread.

MINNOW:
I can't feel anything.

CAT:
You want to take some of my feelings?

MINNOW:
You know what I'm going to tell you to do.

CAT:
No.

MINNOW:
Yes, it always makes you feel better.

CAT:
Well then what's gonna make you feel better.

MINNOW:
Reviewing emergency protocol.

*(*AUDRA *comes back.)*

AUDRA:
Proceed to the exits calmly and quietly.
Minnow makes the emergency call.
We meet up with Clark and Megh / in Centennial Park.

CAT:
Or whoever the bouncers on duty are.

AUDRA:
Exactly.

MINNOW:
Cat's gonna perform.

CAT:
No, they are not.

AUDRA:
Oh, no, you should.
That always makes you feel better.

CAT:
Fine, I'll do it.

AUDRA:
Really?
I get to see it?

MINNOW:
I knew it, I knew you wanted to.

CAT:
Don't make a big DEAL ABOUT IT.

MINNOW:
It's going to be good.
You're going to be so happy you did it.

*(*CAT *puts their forehead to the bar for just a second.*
They look up.
They nod.
They pick up a drink.)

AUDRA:
Put it down.
You don't need it.

*(*AUDRA *takes it from them.*
She gives CAT *a hug.)*

CAT:
Thank you.
(They go to get ready.)

MINNOW:
Did Ariel have any idea what happened?

AUDRA:
No, it was just a fluke.

MINNOW:
Okay
Well.
Shit happens, I guess.

(We shift to the day after.)

TEN

MINNOW:
I feel like an idiot for saying it.
Shit happens.

CAT:
We didn't know what was coming.

AUDRA:
No.
We know too much about what was coming.
What is coming.
This feels like a curse sometimes.
To have a place that everyone knows is for us.

MINNOW:
To have to hold all the ways it could all go sour.
All at one time.
And have to keep going forward.

CAT:
And then not blame ourselves when something happens we didn't
Couldn't prepare for.
You can't prepare for this.

AUDRA:
Not without getting as violent as them.

I don't want to get as violent as them.
I don't want to become like the person who did this.

MINNOW:
And sometimes I can feel myself starting to.
And then I think to myself at least I can feel it happening.
At least I can catch myself before it
Locks in

CAT:
Calcifies.

AUDRA:
I want to stay soft.

(MINNOW and CAT nod.)

AUDRA:
Cat, will you do it again.

CAT:
Which part.

AUDRA:
All of it.

CAT:
I don't think it'll work.

MINNOW:
It worked last night.

CAT:
There is a limit.
I fear this might have reached it.

AUDRA:
Is it at least worth a try?

(CAT nods.)

MINNOW:
You started here.

CAT:
My face

*(They imagine it.
Piece by piece.)*

AUDRA:
Full goth

MINNOW:
The dark feather lashes

AUDRA:
Black stained lips

CAT:
Lower

MINNOW:
That floor length gown of Maggie's that we keep in the back

AUDRA:
The one with the slit all the way up the side

MINNOW:
Morticia Addams glamour.

AUDRA:
Nah
BDSM Wednesday all grown up
Because

AUDRA/CAT:
The closer I get to Wednesday Addams the less I have to smile.

(They share a smile.)

MINNOW:
Black fishnet gloves up to your elbows.

CAT:
The shoes though.

MINNOW/CAT:
Vintage Dior Satin Pumps

MINNOW:
I hadn't seen those out to play in a while

CAT:
They're always in the trunk of my car
Always ready

MINNOW:
You looked—

(Time blurs.)

AUDRA:
Cat what the fuck
You look beautiful
You pulled that together in half an hour?

MINNOW:
Oh my god
You are so fucking handsome??

AUDRA:
Beautiful

MINNOW:
Handsome

AUDRA:
At the same time

MINNOW:
Terrifying

MINNOW/CAT:
Scare the babies

MINNOW:
Whole

AUDRA:
Holy.

MINNOW:
Holy.

(A sharp shift to:)

ELEVEN

CAT:
Holy hell there are so many of you.
You're out so late, way past your bedtime.
Everyone have their glasses?
Raise them.
You can do it.
Up, up, up to the ghosts.
Thank youuuuuuu.
Don't tap your glass to the table,
we want to keep our good ghosts close.
Bring them close to you.
Before you go, let me tell you a little bedtime story.
Is that alright?
(They hold their glass to their chest.)
Okay now—
Some mornings I wake up
and I feel caught in the middle,
feel the she, her, hers, and the he, him, his
waging a war in my gut,
telling my they and them and theirs
that the middle is just muck,
that I must choose.
...
But some mornings I wake up
and it doesn't feel like being stuck at all.
It's something else entirely.
It feels like slipping into warm flannel
and sipping chai while it rains;
some days, fiercer
like slipping feet into

unbroken platform heels,
clusters of muscles in my feet
controlling plantar flexion
feeling the muscles all the way up my leg.
Sometimes it feels like work, but
it takes work to become,
to break in, to settle.
…
On my clearest mornings,
They and them and theirs is a root.
It grounds me so that I can live somewhere
Where the words don't quite reach.
…
I don't know where that leaves me.
I don't want to make a mockery of the women who
Slip feet into soles and find it fuel for their womanness.
Truth be told,
I can be jealous of them.
It's simple for them,
Uncomplicated.
A feeling of being elevated.
They find themselves powerful
but
Heels were made to be unisex.
Travel with me now—
Ninth century.
Persian men wore heels into battle on horseback:
A symbol of wealth
Of manliness.
Brought them to the courts of Europe
Where courtesans thought perhaps they could feel elevated, too.
Slipping feet into shoes
Is me preparing for the battle of being
Fighting
Ritual

It's the last thing I do before stepping on stage.
It roots me to things that came long before me,
Like if I had the means to trace up my family tree
Could I find a member of the some cavalry that shares
my name? That maybe also felt between
and outside?
Who in one perfect breath found themselves—lifted.
...
I tattooed a Persian Cedar tree on my thigh the day
before I turned twenty-one.
I held hands with myself,
clutched my own body for the two hours it took for the
needle to leave all of the ink beneath my
skin.
Dipping in and out faster than hummingbird wings
Watched as my artist poured their heart into my flesh
And I asked how long they'd been tattooing.
They looked young but they said twenty years.

And I said I couldn't imagine doing anything for
twenty years.
And they winked when they said
It roots me.
And we laughed,
And I studied the hard edges of their face
The shadows of a red beard creeping in
as they smiled and said the art of creating,
it makes me feel so feminine, you know?
and I said
I know
Because I did
And they said
The queer in me recognizes the queer in you
Like a beacon,
like a lighthouse.
The fresh ink in my thigh leaving a dull throbbing
reminder

a steady pulse of knowing
It didn't matter what I looked like to anyone else
I could claim my femaleness
And I could claim my maleness
They could exist together
And I could be complete
…
I went back to the same artist five years later
And I looked different
I looked more—
Me.
And they said
I'd know you anywhere.
I was wondering what happened to you.
It's so good to know you're still
here
And they put a lighthouse on my other thigh
Tall and strong like a cedar tree.
…
So I keep slipping my feet into shoes
Where I can see my entire existence snap into sharp
focus.
And I keep painting my face
Covering up my brows
Glittering my lips
Extending my lashes so far
Past the clouds
and past the stars
and out of Florida
out of fucking Florida
and back in time
Lashes long enough to butterfly kiss
Marsha
and Sylvia
and the femmes who came before me
the ones who yelled at the cops
in the languages they spoke at home with their

mothers.
I want to feel the asphalt of Christopher Street under one foot
And the floor of Gene Compton's under the other
A brick in one hand
A cup of coffee in the other.
The whole expanse of the United States in my lungs
All the queer kids screaming at once
Calling across time and space
To all the good ghosts—
I want to thank them for the air I breathe
deeper and deeper
And deeper
And deeper and deeper,
Thank them for the way they stood among the sharpest of rocks
And called out to me with such radiant light.

*(*CAT *takes the shot.*
We shift.)

TWELVE

MINNOW:
Mmm.
It was never the building.

AUDRA:
Not even for a moment.

CAT:
It's always been us.

MINNOW:
And we're okay

AUDRA:
We're okay

CAT:
We're okay

MINNOW:
This room is just walls and doors.
To be walked through and knocked down.
We're just a little blue pocket in a little red city
In a purple swing state
In a clusterfuck experiment of togetherness
We aren't inherently safe.
Not even close.
Not alone.
But if I look out for you.
And you look out for me.

CAT:
No one left behind.

MINNOW:
Keep showing up as the people we are.
Even when just showing up is the hardest thing in the world.

AUDRA:
No hiding.

MINNOW:
I will lace your fingers through mine
Because I know you would do the same for me
And I will tell you that you are
complete
And you are beautiful
and you are strong
and that you being your most you
makes me want to be my most me.
And good god, isn't that freeing?

AUDRA:
All I want these days is laced fingers
Reminding me that you're here next to me.

CAT:
And laced boots
Keeping us grounded.
(They lace their fingers together.)

MINNOW:
I swear to you both here and now that I'll keep trying to keep you safe.

AUDRA:
I swear to you both
here and now
That I'll keep trying to keep you safe.

CAT:
I swear to you both here and now that I'll keep trying to keep you safe.

(A breath)

MINNOW:
Some time tonight, we let everyone know what we need to finish cleaning this place up.
Tomorrow, we can play some music and let everyone help.
Throw a little party.
But today.
Right now.
I need a cup of coffee.

AUDRA:
Let's go.
Let's get out of here.

CAT:
Go where.

AUDRA:
The water.

MINNOW/CAT:
The water.

(They start to gather their things and leave.)

CAT:
It's going to be freezing.

AUDRA:
We don't have to go *in*.
We could find a restaurant on the bay and have a drink.

MINNOW:
Drink somewhere other than here?

AUDRA:
Blasphemous, I know.

CAT:
Okay, hear me out.
What if we drive out to Frida's.

MINNOW:
You want to drive to *Largo* right now?

CAT:
It's like a *second* away from the beach.
We can get sandwiches and take them to the water.

AUDRA:
No, we could go to the place on Anna Maria where the tables are in the sand.
We might as well, we've got all this time.

*(*CAT *and* AUDRA *leave.*
MINNOW *hangs back for a moment.*
She looks at the room one last time.
She turns the lights off.)

END OF PLAY

www.ingramcontent.com/pod-product-compliance
Ingram Content Group UK Ltd.
Pitfield, Milton Keynes, MK11 3LW, UK
UKHW022007190726
13853UKWH00004B/1778

9 798888 560464